To Be Complete

30 DAYS TO OVERCOMING THE WOUNDS OF A TOXIC RELATIONSHIP

Vasti Loredo

Franklin Publishing

PRINCETON, TEXAS

Kelly Carr / Franklin Publishing
1215 Juniper
Princeton, Texas 75407

www.FranklinPublishing.org

Ordering Information:

Quantity sales. Special discounts are available on quantity purchases by corporations, associations, and others. For details, contact the "Special Sales Department" at the address above.

To Be Complete: 30 Days To Overcoming The Wounds Of A Toxic Relationship / Vasti Loredo. —1st ed.

Published by Franklin Publishing, Princeton, Texas.

Printed in the United States of America, 2020.

All rights reserved.
ISBN-10: 1-7320028-9-4
ISBN-13: 978-1-7320028-9-0

Testimonials

"Vasti Loredo is a wonderful young lady, mother, Life Coach, and alumni of MLCTI. I believe every young lady around the world should read her book, *To Be Complete!* This will be one book that they will want to keep for the rest of their lives and pass on what they learn from it to other young ladies they mentor including daughters and granddaughters."
Rodney Love, President, Master Life Coach Training Institute, www.MasterLifeCoachInstitute.com

"*To Be Complete* is a spiritual guide to any young lady traveling through a journey of healing and restoration. It is a dose of grace for anyone who seems too far out of reach. In this devotional, Vasti shares such a vulnerable and transparent part of her life and journey that I'd hoped years ago could have been available to me in my most trying seasons."
Pastor Letty Garcia, La Nueva Jerusalem Church, Andrews, Texas

"Insightful. Honest. Beautiful. Vasti's personal journey, a living testimony for all young ladies in need of wisdom and guidance in relationships. I love how the Lord has healed her and turned this story of pain and brokenness into joy and peace. Establishing a firm foundation rooted in Christ, Vasti has enabled for all women to find their voice and to stand up strongly in midst of difficult relationships and to fully put one's faith in our Lord and Savior, Jesus Christ. This is a call to action to not settle for scraps and to respect one's boundaries and to wait patiently in God even when the going gets tough. He works everything according to His good plan for all those who love and willingly obey Him and want to find true joy and peace. He is the Author of Love."
Maileny Villegas.

"I found this book so encouraging and uplifting. It ministered to my heart. As I read these devotionals each one spoke to different areas of my heart; to have faith, to not grow bitter, to find true completeness in God! It both made me cry and filled me with hope. I truly enjoyed it and can't wait to share a copy with others. Thank you!"
Diana Montes, Youth Minister

Dedication

This book is lovingly dedicated to my parents, Ricardo and Vicky, and to my son Jonathan. You are my support and my motivation. I love you.

Contents

PREFACE

I was 17 years old when I naively entered my first, serious, romantic relationship. Initially, it was everything I had dreamed it would be. He was charming, handsome, and he gave me the attention I yearned for. I was certain this would be my fairytale. I felt like I deserved it and nothing could go wrong. However, it wasn't long before I was living in a nightmare of pain, insecurity, and emotional abuse.

I was afraid to tell anyone what was really going on because I feared I would lose him. I knew I wanted to get out of the relationship, but the soul ties were too strong for me to just get up and walk away. So, I endured, hoping it would eventually get better. I tried to keep up the image of a good Christian girl who knew what she was doing. Nonetheless, the people that loved me eventually started to sense that things were not right. I ignored concerns from practically everyone around me. Stubborn to make things "work out" and afraid to be left in shame and heartbreak, I traded all my healthy relationships for the *one* that was tearing me apart. I thought that maybe every relationship went through a season like the one I was going through. With time, things only became worse and my self-esteem and self-value plummeted. After 4 years, it was finally over, ending with more pain and regret than I knew was possible. I knew I had to make a change in my life.

It was the beginning of a new year and I decided I was done with the old and wanted a fresh start. I was broken, but I was ready to let God restore me. Little did I know that I was carrying a child in my womb. Desperate and afraid, I thought my world had come to an end. How could I heal now, if I was going to be connected to the very man that had broken me? How could I reach my goals and dreams as a single mom? I could not understand what God was doing and I could not see that this was the beginning of my healing journey.

With a new responsibility, I knew that I could not give up and wallow in depression. I had to pick up the pieces of my life and surrender them completely to God. If I was ever going to be a good mother, I had to learn to put God first, depending entirely on Him for everything. My contentment and self-worth had to come from Him. Before, I only thought those things came from a man. Now, God was opening up my eyes to the truth. He was getting me out of my comfort zone in order to grow. I began praying and searching God's word for direction and healing. I found comfort in hearing godly women like Nancy Leigh DeMoss and Dannah Gresh. I read their books and listened to their teachings wherever I could find them. Then, I began writing my own thoughts down, as if I were writing to myself from the outside looking in.

This devotional came from those beautiful, sometimes painful moments of raw honesty, vulnerability, and complete surrender to God. I had to learn to let go of so many things, all while being open to God's will for my life.

It is my desire that you may feel the love of God as you read the words written in this book, by a girl who was once very broken, but who found restoration and healing in the arms of Jesus. I cannot say that the journey has been easy, nor can I promise you smooth sailing as you embark on this healing journey. Nonetheless, what I can do is remind you of His promises and His redeeming love. Within the pages of this book, you will find the treasure of God's word reminding you that He is with you. No matter what you have been through, you can trust that you are safe and complete in His arms. Only He can make you whole.

Vasti Loredo
April, 2020

Day 1
You Are Not Alone

Psalm 139:1-6

1 O LORD, You have searched me and known me.
2 You know my sitting down and my rising up;
You understand my thought afar off.
3 You comprehend my path and my lying down,
And are acquainted with all my ways.
4 For there is not a word on my tongue, But be-
hold, O LORD, You know it altogether.
5 You have hedged me behind and before, And
laid Your hand upon me.
6 Such knowledge is too wonderful for me; It is
high, I cannot attain it.

There are so many lies that can overtake the heart and mind of a person that is stuck in a destructive relationship. Convincing lies such as, "you are un-loved" or "your situation is hopeless," always seem to linger. These lies don't loosen their grip just because you are no longer in that relationship. They can continue to stab at your heart and whisper into your thoughts long after the relationship has ended.

One of the biggest lies that affects so many bro-ken-hearted people, is the lie that shouts, "You are alone." The truth is, you are not alone, and you never have been. God has been there, but at times we are the ones who turn away from Him. When we turn to Him, He reveals His truth to us through His Word and things begin to change.

Right now, you might be battling with feelings of loneliness. Perhaps, you are feeling unworthy and forgotten. Even so, God is letting know through His Word today, that He knows you. He understands what you've been through, and He has His hand upon you. He is with you. It can be difficult to believe these words because of the pain you have endured. However, it is vital that you begin the steps to healing by surrendering your heart to God through Jesus Christ, and believing that you are not alone. God is walking right next to you as you begin the journey to healing and freedom.

God held me through the worst of my breakup, giving me His strength in my weakest moments. I was ashamed to express my conflicting feelings to anyone. Honestly, at times I couldn't understand them myself. I knew it would be difficult to understand why I missed him so much. Wasn't he the one that caused me so much pain? Yet here I was crying over him and feeling the ache of his absence. It did not make sense, yet I knew God understood every detail of my heartbreak, as He understands yours. Trust Him, He will get you through whatever you are facing today.

Prayer

Dear God. I have felt alone for so long. I have felt completely forgotten and helpless. But Your word says that You know my sitting down and rising up. You know me and understand me. Your word says You have Your hand upon me. You are taking care of my life. I want to believe and trust You. I surrender my life to You. Without You I cannot go on. Please help me in my weaknesses, and comfort me through the pain that is still very present in my heart. In the name of Jesus, I pray. Amen

Questions for Reflection

1. How has loneliness affected the decisions you have made in the past?

2. Do you feel that dwelling on the past has affected your ability to let go of guilt and pain?

3. How easy or difficult is it for you to read God's Word and His promises, and believe that those are meant for you?

Day 2
You Are Forgiven

Psalm 130:1-4

1 Out of the depths I have cried to You, O LORD;
2 Lord, hear my voice! Let Your ears be attentive
To the voice of my supplications.
3 If You, LORD, should mark iniquities, O Lord,
who could stand?
4 But there is forgiveness with You, That You
may be feared.

There are days when the memories are overwhelming, and the shame is blinding. The lies come again, telling you that it's all your fault, making you fall into the trap of replaying memories over and over. Guilt can pierce the soul mercilessly but thank God for His mercy. The past is gone now and that which was blamed on you, rightfully or not, has been erased. If you have asked God to forgive you, He already has. The problem is, at times we cannot forgive ourselves. Sometimes we hold on to guilt that should not exist.

If you have endured someone blaming you time after time, even for things that were not your fault, it's hard to accept forgiveness. God is not condemning you. The word of God says that He will have compassion on us and cast our sins into the depths of the sea (Micah 7:19). Jesus died to redeem you and give you new life.

As a child of God, there is no need to live in shame. I know it's easier said than done, but it is possible. If you have been holding on to guilt so tightly that it has almost become a normal part of you, The Lord wants to take that burden from you today. All it takes is a humble and repented heart. Sincerely ask Him to free you and believe that by faith in Jesus Christ and the price that He has already paid for you, you are forgiven.

Prayer

Dear God, I come to You humbly, asking for forgiveness. I know You are faithful and You keep Your Word, so I thank You for forgiving of all my sins. At times I have felt so guilty and ashamed. But I know Your Word says that You have forgiven me, and You do not remember my sin anymore. Help me now to forgive myself and to let go of the guilt that often plagues me. I ask that You shield my thoughts from dwelling on the past. Like the Psalm says, please be attentive to the voice of my supplications. I need You. I'm the name of Jesus, I pray. Amen.

Questions for Reflection

1. Are their certain things or occasions that trigger memories for you, and what are some ways you can redirect those thoughts?

(quoting scripture, intentionally closing out certain thought as soon as they start, etc.)

2. Has the burden of holding on to the past kept you from pursuing new things?

Day 3
You Were Made with a Purpose

Psalm 139:13-17

13 For You formed my inward parts; You covered me in my mother's womb.
14 I will praise You, for I am fearfully and wonderfully made; Marvelous are Your works, And that my soul knows very well.
15 My frame was not hidden from You, When I was made in secret, And skillfully wrought in the lowest parts of the earth.
16 Your eyes saw my substance, being yet unformed. And in Your book they all were written, The days fashioned for me, When as yet there were none of them.
17 How precious also are Your thoughts to me, O God! How great is the sum of them!

The beauty of these passages is healing water to the anguished soul. To know that you were made with a wonderful purpose by the marvelous Creator of the universe, is something too great to understand. He took the time to skillfully form every detail of your being, and He wrote your story in His book.

His thoughts of you are precious. How special! How extraordinary! You're not just randomly existing without a reason. God created you purposely. You may be wondering, "Why then have I suffered so much? Why then has my life taken so many negative turns?" The truth is, we live in world where evil exists. Sin intrudes into the plans God has for us. But all is not lost. When you give God permission to be the Lord of your life and renounce the sin that separates you from Him, no matter what happens, you can trust that He will fulfill His great plans in your life.

You may suffer from low self-esteem as a result of being in a detrimental relationship, but God wants to take that away. He wants you to understand the beauty of the life He gave you. He formed you with a meaningful purpose and nothing that has happened to you, nothing that anyone has done to you, can take that away. Your past does not change the fact that you were wonderfully made. All the spoken hurtful words that have made you feel inadequate, cannot erase your value as a child of God. Let the lies fade away and let God's word speak truth to your life.

Prayer

Dear God, You are The Creator of all beautiful things. Your word says You created me. You knew me even before I was conceived. I cannot fathom such beauty. If I am honest, sometimes it's hard for me to believe that I was made for a great purpose. My heart has been trampled on and I have felt so belittled. Help me to believe that I am valuable. Help me to know that I am worth so much to You. In the name of Jesus, I pray. Amen.

Questions for Reflection

1. What are some of the dreams and goals you had for yourself in the past, that you have put aside because of the toxic relationship?

2. Are their certain lies that were spoken over you, that you have been subconsciously holding onto and believing about yourself?

3. The word of God is full of truths about who you really are. He says you are chosen, beloved, and much more. What specific truths from the Word of God can you use to knock down each lie?

Day 4
Healing

Isaiah 55:1-3

1 "Ho! Everyone who thirsts, Come to the waters; And you who have no money, Come, buy and eat. Yes, come, buy wine and milk Without money and without price.
2 Why do you spend money for what is not bread, And your wages for what does not satisfy? Listen carefully to Me, and eat what is good, And let your soul delight itself in abundance.
3 Incline your ear, and come to Me. Hear, and your soul shall live; And I will make an everlasting covenant with you-- The sure mercies of David.

Making the decision to leave a hurtful relationship is not a simple choice. There is a lot of pain involved during and after the process. From loneliness to doubt, there are many different emotions that can flood your heart. You might even question if you made the right choice. At times you may even feel withdrawal symptoms, like wanting to go back, questioning if it was really "that bad." It's something no one can understand unless they have been through it.

However, your situation is not hopeless. God is giving you an invitation to bring your tired soul to Him, and allow Him to quench your thirst. When the scripture speaks of wine and milk, it's not physically referring to the tangible liquid. It's talking about nutrition for your spirit, that only comes from God Himself. He no longer wants you to spend your "money," which can mean your emotions and time, on what does not satisfy. Nothing else will fill the void that's left in your heart. Only Jesus can give you the true joy that you've longed for, for all these years.

Many times, we are used to giving and giving only to receive criticism and rejection in return. God's invitation will not leave you empty. If you come to Him, heart surrendered, He will in return satisfy your heart with His abundance.

God says in His word, "...come to Me. Hear. And your soul shall live." There is new life in God. There is healing in His arms. His Word says, "Come buy and eat...without money without price..." You may have nothing more than a broken heart to offer God. That's okay because He gives us grace freely. There's nothing we can give or do to repay His goodness. He just asks that we take His invitation and follow Him. He is the Bread of Life.

Prayer

Dear God, I realize that You are the only living water and You are the bread of life. I've spent my time and energy on things that did not satisfy. I was disillusioned when nothing could fill my void. I now come to You, thirsty and hungry for a change. Heal my brokenness. Close these wounds. Quench my thirst and help me trust in You. I don't want to return to a hurtful relationship. Please remove all feelings of confusion and doubt from my heart. Restore my soul and make an everlasting covenant with me. In the name of Jesus. Amen.

Questions for Reflection

1. The scripture asks "Why do you spend money on what is not bread?" Money can refer to your time, emotions, and so many other things that you have the ability to give. What things were you spending your "money" on, before you found the Bread of Life?

2. Are your past experiences affecting the way you respond to God's invitation?

Day 5
You Can Trust God

Jeremiah 29:11-13

11 For I know the thoughts that I think toward you, says the LORD, thoughts of peace and not of evil, to give you a future and a hope.
12 Then you will call upon Me and go and pray to Me, and I will listen to you.
13 And you will seek Me and find Me, when you search for Me with all your heart.

Each time someone lets you down, your trust becomes smaller. Each time you are lied to or hurt; your heart builds up walls for protection. You know it all too well from experience, that unsettling insecurity that comes as a result of being in an abusive relationship.

I remember how it tore me up inside not knowing if I was really loved, the sense of not feeling good enough, and being weighed down with so many other doubts. But did you know that God will never let you down? Stop and reflect upon that statement. He will never lie to you. He will never hurt you. Can you say this about anyone else? We all know the answer to that is "No."

This does not mean you won't have pain. We live in a world full of sin. It is inevitable. But in God you can experience peace and security even through the pain. These are priceless gifts that I think we can all agree we did not have when we were in a destructive relationship. You don't have to worry about broken promises because He will come through for each one. You no longer have to try to be good enough, because He already paid the price for you. You are already precious to Him. There is no need to doubt His love. Isn't that what we all long to find? Isn't that what we've searched for?

Pause and take moment to meditate on this truth. It's going to be okay if you trust God. He has wonderful plans for your life. But He wants you to call out to Him. Seek Him with all your heart. He promises to be by your side. He stands at the door and knocks, ready to be the Lord of your life, but only you can let Him in. Believe His word. You can trust Him.

Prayer

Dear God, Thank You for Your promises of hope. Thank you because You care enough about me that You take time to speak to me. Your Word says You know the plans that You have for me, plans to give me hope and a future. I embrace Your Word today and I put my trust in You Jesus. You died on the cross to give me new life, to forgive my sins, and to heal my wounds. You gave me Your Word to guide me through life, through the good and bad. I hold tight to Your promises. Help me to put my trust only in You. In the name of Jesus, I pray. Amen.

Questions for Reflection

1. Can you identify any obstacles that are keeping you from truly trusting God?

2. In what ways have you seen God's faithfulness this week?

Day 6
Let Go of Your Worries

Philippians 4:6-7

6 Be anxious for nothing, but in everything by prayer and supplication, with thanksgiving, let your requests be made known to God;
7 and the peace of God, which surpasses all understanding, will guard your hearts and minds through Christ Jesus.

What are the worries that occupy your mind the most? Do you worry about being alone? Do you worry that the hurt in your heart will never heal or that you will always have attachments to your ex? Maybe you are still going through issues with him and are unsure of the choices you have made?

Whatever your worries are, God wants to give you peace and confidence in the midst of your circumstance. He wants you to turn to Him with whatever is burdening you. There is a solution to everything. And while you might not get an answer overnight, keep trusting in The Lord. He has perfect timing. So, do not be anxious or worried. Pray about your struggles and worries.

Ask for that peace that surpasses all understanding. Let Him take the worry from you and let His peace guard your heart and mind from all doubt and fear. Don't second guess the choice you have made to begin the healing journey for yourself. Simply be patient and pray. Share you heart with God today. He wants to hear what's on your mind. He cares for you.

Lastly, give Him thanks. A grateful heart can change your outlook on life. In His infinite wisdom, God tells us to give thanks. Why? Because when we shift our focus from problems to blessings, it brings hope and peace. Suddenly a problem that was preventing a peaceful sleep at night, seems so minor compared to the blessing of having salvation, being safe, and knowing you are loved.

It does not mean everything in life will be perfect. Problems come and go, people come and go, but there is always something to be grateful for. It may sound cliché, but if you really give it thought and apply it to your life, you will see the beauty in gratefulness. If we meditate on our blessings and recognize that every good thing comes from God (James 1:17), we can appreciate even the tiniest of blessings.

Prayer

Dear God, You know all things. You see the future and You have the solution to everything. God, I am burdened with worry and it's weighing me down. I come to You as Your Word instructs. Take these worries from me. I trust You will help me get through this. Give me that peace that surpasses all understanding. I don't want to worry about the things I cannot change. Do Your perfect will in my life because that's really all that matters. Help me appreciate the blessings You have given me. Thank You for the work You are doing in my life. In the name of Jesus, I pray. Amen.

Questions for Reflection

1. What are some of the worries that are weighing you down today, and are you ready to start praying about them rather than just dwelling on them?

2. If tomorrow you lost everything that you have never thanked God for, what are some of the things you would not have any more?

Day 7
God Is for You

Romans 8:31-32

31 What then shall we say to these things? If God is for us, who can be against us?
32 He who did not spare His own Son, but delivered Him up for us all, how shall He not with Him also freely give us all things?

There is a daily battle that arises each day when we wake up. It starts in the mind and from there continues with different situations that we face. The enemy can disguise himself in many different forms, using people, situations, emotions, and even thoughts. When these things come to attack you, when certain people you thought you could trust hurt you, and when you feel alone, just know that God is for you. He will strengthen you. He is fighting the battle for you if you allow Him to. We cannot do it alone.

After leaving a bad relationship, you are extremely vulnerable to fall when the enemy comes to attack. This is why you must cling to God. How? Fill your heart and mind with His word and truth. Claim the promises He has given you. Seek Him in prayer with all your heart. He loves you so much that He gave His only Son in ransom for your life. He will give you what you need if you trust in Him. Believe that if He is on your side, nothing can defeat you. You may fall, you may hurt, but God will ultimately have the victory and He will protect you. Meditate on this word throughout your day and believe that The Lord is on your side.

Prayer

Dear God, Thank You for giving Your Son Jesus to die on the cross for me so that I could live. It was the greatest sacrifice. If You did that for me, then it's clear, Your love is beyond amazing. Lord help me with these daily battles. Deliver me from the enemy's hand. Because if You are for me, nothing can come against me. This is all possible because You are God and You love me. Help me to stay firm in Your truth and continue in Your path. Thank You Father. In the name of Jesus, I pray. Amen.

Questions for Reflection

1. Can you identify the different battles that you are facing right now, mentally or physically?

2. What are some things you can start doing differently in order to trust God with your problems?

Day 8
Everything Will Work Out for Good

Romans 8:28

28 And we know that all things work together for good to those who love God, to those who are the called according to His purpose.

Regret. Why did I allow myself to be treated like that? Why didn't I leave sooner? I wish I would have done things differently. Maybe if I would have given him another chance, he would have changed.

All these thoughts and many more have probably invaded your mind a number of times. But we cannot change the past, and we certainly cannot change a person. Only God can do that. Right now, you are where you are for a reason. God wants to heal you and redirect your life. Everything that has happened in your past can affect you in one of two ways. You can let it have a negative impact on your life, letting self-pity take over, eventually running into another bad relationship, seeking validation from empty sources. Or you can let God mold you and work everything out for the better. Your scars can be a reminder of God's mercy. Your experience can give you wisdom for future decisions, preventing you from repeating those same mistakes again. Moreover, you can live with gratitude that God has rescued you and rendered His forgiveness to you.

Everything will fall into place because God promises to work out everything for good to those that love Him. You might not understand how your situation can be turned into something good, but know that God is sovereign and in time, you will see His plan begin to unfold in front of you. Then you will understand how your troubles and heart ache played a part in molding and strengthening you for greater purposes.

Prayer

Dear God, I realize I cannot change the past and I don't hold the power to change a person. So, I ask You to take this from my hands and help me let go of all regret. I want Your will in my life and I want You to turn all this mess into something beautiful. I can't see the future, but You can. I give You control of my life so that You can lead me into tomorrow with certainty and love. In the name of Jesus. Amen.

Questions for Reflection

1. Think of some good things that have come out of the painful situation you have faced. Ask yourself these questions. Are you stronger

now? Is your relationship with God improving? Are you feeling safe now?

2. What is one good thing that you are hoping will come out of all this once you are further along in your healing journey?

Day 9
When You Don't Know
What to Say

Romans 8:26-27

26 Likewise the Spirit also helps in our weaknesses. For we do not know what we should pray for as we ought, but the Spirit Himself makes intercession for us with groanings which cannot be uttered.
27 Now He who searches the hearts knows what the mind of the Spirit is, because He makes intercession for the saints according to the will of God.-

The weakness that comes after a traumatic breakup is indescribable. For me, it was a feeling of a fearful dead end. My body literally felt sick. I did not know what would happen next. It really did feel like the end. Somedays it was hard to pray.

Right now, life may seem uncertain and you may not even be able to understand your own feelings. The world seems blurry and you aren't sure what to do next. Even praying may seem difficult because you might not know what to ask for or what to say. That's why this scripture offers so much comfort. The Spirit will intercede for you according to God's will.

God knows what you need. His will for your life is better than anything else, including your own will and your own plans. All you have to do is be willing. Take time for prayer and pour out your heart to God. If you find that you don't know what to say, just be sincere and let God take over. Trust that the Spirit of God intercedes for you. Trust that He comes through for His children in their weaknesses. When we are weak, He is strong (2 Cor 12:9).

Prayer

Dear God, I want to thank You for sustaining me. I know You will never leave me. I want to trust that You have everything under control. But often, I feel unsure and afraid of the future. At times I don't even know what I really need, but You do. So, I ask that Your Holy Spirit intercede for me. Do Your perfect will in my life. I let go of my own will and my own plans. I ask for Your guidance. Help my heart to keep healing, and fulfill the longings of my heart according to Your will. In the name of Jesus, I pray. Amen.

Questions for Reflection

1. Has your heart been so full of emotions that it has become difficult to express yourself in prayer?

2. Now that you know that the Spirit of God Himself intercedes for you during the moments you need it most, how does this change or strengthen your view of prayer?

Day 10
The Year of Drought

Jeremiah 17:7-8

7 *"Blessed is the man who trusts in the LORD, And whose hope is the LORD.*
8 *For he shall be like a tree planted by the waters, Which spreads out its roots by the river, And will not fear when heat comes; But its leaf will be green, And will not be anxious in the year of drought, Nor will cease from yielding fruit.*

I remember when he was my everything. Maybe I did not want to admit it, but I couldn't imagine life without him. Instead of God, it was him, the man who did not respect me, care for me, or even truly love me. But there I was putting my trust in him, hoping for a better outcome than the one I was getting. Nonetheless, my heart remained empty. Can you relate to my situation?

God invites us to put our trust and hope in Him. He won't let you down. Like a tree full of life that drinks from the running river, He will satisfy the thirst within you. You might be afraid to let go and trust God because of all the time and emotions you have invested in someone else. Even so, The Word of God assures us that you will be blessed if you put your hope and trust in The Lord. And through this drought that you may seem to be passing through, God will be there to nourish and strengthen you. The Word says that even when the heat comes, your leaf will be green, meaning that, though the painful trials may come, God will keep giving you life and strength. What more could a broken heart ask for, but the comfort and love from The Creator Himself.

Remember, you cannot get through this alone. You need God. You need His direction, lest you return to where you came from and sink deeper into a life away from Him.

Prayer

Dear God, As I walk through this drought, my heart feels tired. I know I need to trust in You, but at times it seems difficult. Forgive me for my doubt. Please help me to keep my hope in You Jesus. I want to trust You with everything. Plant me as a tree near the waters. Spread my roots into the river. Calm my fears and anxiety. Let the leaves of my tree be green even through the droughts in my life. Let Your hope always be present in my life. I need to realize that You know what is best for me. I don't want to make my own decisions anymore. Instead I want to be directed by Your Spirit. Please fill me with Your Holy Spirit and be my guide. My hope and trust are in You. In the name of Jesus, I pray. Amen.

Questions for Reflection

1. For you personally, what has been one of the hardest parts about letting go of a relationship that you have invested so much into?

2. Are there any areas in your life that you are still withholding from God due to lack of trust?

3. Do you believe God will redeem all of your wasted years and give you wholeness in exchange for your trust and obedience?

Day 11
Heart

Jeremiah 17:9

9 "The heart is deceitful above all things, And desperately wicked; Who can know it?

The truth is, you cannot "follow your heart." Yes, I know it is what we have been taught from a young age. Our culture has embraced it as a truth and a guarantee for happiness. However, it continues to be an erroneous way of thinking. We've all been led astray by our hearts. Our emotions have at times betrayed us, and its possibly why many young women end up in abusive relationships. The heart swears it is in love, when in reality it's a mixture of compromise, insecurities, infatuation, and the need to fill a deeper void. The heart keeps people in cycles of pain hoping for a better outcome. The heart that is not led by God can lead you to destruction.

Now that you have made the decision to walk away from that relationship, your heart is going to be flooded with many emotions. Don't be surprised if you suddenly, desperately wish you were back with that person who hurt you so much. You might start painfully missing them, and even start belittling the abuse you went through. You may begin blaming yourself for why things went downhill, but remember, the heart is deceitful. Going back to that type of relationship is not the solution. It is never acceptable to allow someone to keep hurting you emotionally, physically, sexually, or mentally. And it is not okay to blame yourself for the abuse. Whatever your heart may be telling you today, or whatever mind-battle you are going through, put it in God's hands. Ask the Lord to help you clear your mind of confusing thoughts. Ask for His direction before letting your heart lead you astray.

Prayer

Dear God, I thank you for being by my side. Lord, more than ever I desperately need You. I am vulnerable and my heart is full of confusing emotions. Please don't let me be led astray by my heart. Take control and give me peace about my situation. Sometimes I feel lost and I want to do things on my own, but God I want to give You control of my life. I know Your ways are better than mine. I trust You. Lead me oh God, lead my heart. In the name of Jesus, I pray. Amen.

Questions for Reflection

1. Can you look back on your life now and recognize the times that your heart led you in the wrong direction?

2. Before following your heart the next time you have an impulse, what can you do to make sure it is a wise, God-honoring decision?

Day 12
The Future

Matthew 6:31-33

31 Therefore do not worry, saying, 'What shall we eat?' or 'What shall we drink?' or 'What shall we wear?'
32 For after all these things the Gentiles seek. For your heavenly Father knows that you need all these things.
33 But seek first the kingdom of God and His righteousness, and all these things shall be added to you.

It's so easy to get caught up in worrying about the future, especially since breaking off an abusive relationship can be a drastic change. It can leave you wondering, "What's next?" You've probably been so used to living your life entwined with this other person and all your plans have revolved around them. Now, taking one step forward without them can leave you feeling uncertain about your future. It's only normal that we go through these phases. However, you do not have to settle for hopelessness and insecurity.

God knows what you need in order to continue. You may be unsure, but He is sure. You may feel weak, but He is strong. Don't worry about what you have or don't have, or how you will get to where you want to be. Don't worry about how you will make it through. Take it one day at a time. Ask God to help you get through today before worrying about tomorrow. In these passages, Jesus tells us to seek first His kingdom. What does that consist of? We can start by focusing on Him, reading and living His word, and believing His promises for our lives. Then we can trust that He will provide for our needs, spiritually, physically, and emotionally.

Prayer

Dear God, Thank You for Your provision. You have never left me even if at times I could not feel You. Help me to trust that You will keep providing for my every need. At times I worry if I will be able to make it through. Lord You know I need strength and healing. You know that I also have earthly needs. Even those things which I don't know I need, You know them well. Help me to trust You so that this burden of worry would be lifted off of my shoulders. Help me learn to seek Your kingdom first. I know You will be faithful. In the name of Jesus, I pray. Amen.

Questions for Reflection

1. This past week, where did you put more energy into, worrying about problems, or seeking the kingdom of God?

2. Can you think about the past times when God made a way through difficult situations? Even if you did not know or trust Him then, the blessings you enjoyed were all a result of His mercy. Can you recognize when God is blessing you?

Day 13
Separated No More

Ephesians 2:13

13 But now in Christ Jesus you who once were far off have been brought near by the blood of Christ.

I continue to see that one of the major things that plagues the victims of abuse, is loneliness. The isolation that comes with having an abusive partner can feel unbearable. It's that feeling of being in a crowd, and feeling completely out of place and unconnected, wanting an escape but feeling too distant and trapped to trust anyone with your feelings.

The problem is, when you get out of a relationship like that, the loneliness does not retire immediately. It can actually become so much stronger and overpowering, causing anxiety. In that desperation, your heart can be inclined to either return to the one who hurt you or lead you astray into another relationship. Neither of these two are the answer.

The reason our hearts can fall into this state of desperation, is because we are missing something. You might feel that you are missing that certain person, but what you really need is to fill the void with the fullness of Jesus. Only He can make you whole. He is the only One who can restore you and mend you back together.

Jesus paid the price to remove all obstacles that keep us from Him. The main obstacle, sin, puts a barrier between us and God (Isaiah 59:2). But because of the price He paid and the blood He shed, we can come to Him, repented, desperate, broken, and He will draw us near. If we allow Him to, He will begin to restore us through His Word and Holy Spirit. Just like the scripture says, we were once far off, and distant from Him, but He made a way for us to be near to Him.

He's calling you today to surrender to Him. He will draw you near if you let Him. I know your trust has probably been shattered, and fear has ruled in your life for quite some time. Today, however, you can let go of that fear. You can trust that He wants to change your lonely heart into a beautiful, mended work of art. Let Him draw you near today.

Prayer

Dear God, I know You see my desperate heart and the loneliness that surrounds me at times. There are moments when it feels so heavy. You know I can't go on like this. Draw me near, I need You. Take these burdens from me. Complete me so that my heart won't long for anyone else. Take the desperation out of my heart. Satisfy my thirsty soul. No one else can fill me like You can. I trust You with my life. Take control of it. I put it in your hands. Forgive me because I realize that in the past I have put things and people before You. All along, You should have been my priority. Help me see that only in You, I can be made whole. In the name of Jesus. Amen.

Questions for Reflection

1. What are some things you automatically run to when you feel lonely?

2. Are you willing to make a shift and run to God instead?

Day 14
Power in Confession

James 5:16

16 Confess your trespasses to one another, and pray for one another, that you may be healed. The effective, fervent prayer of a righteous man avails much.

I never realized how much weight I was carrying emotionally and mentally, until I finally had the courage to trust someone and confess everything to that person. The devastation of the break-up I was going through, led me to make a path-changing decision, and it was the best decision I could have made. I decided to let God set me free.

I have come to realize that He set up this principle of confessing our sins and secrets to one another in order to begin the work of freedom in our lives. God is light and when everything comes out to light, there is freedom. There is room to grow. There is accountability.

The opposite is also true. Satan wants to keep you in darkness, hiding secrets, holding back truth, pretending to be okay. Even if you don't realize it,

secrets and lies hold you prisoner. You don't realize how much you're holding back until you let go.

The relief of sharing your story and confessing
the dark pains and secrets in your life, can be so re-
lieving that even your physical body rests. We all
have regrets and things that we are too ashamed to
talk about, but there is rest and freedom in confes-
sion.

First, God wants us to confess our sins to Him,
and to trust Him with everything we've been hiding. He already knows it, but He wants us to take
the first step. Next, the best thing you can do, is
find someone who loves God, loves you, and who
wants to help you through this rough season. You
might feel that you don't know anyone whom you
can really trust.

The truth is that sometimes we don't realize that
the people who care and love us, are the ones sur-
rounding us. We have just been too isolated for so
long to see it. Mothers, sisters, church leaders,
friends, they are there. Sometimes you just need to
let them know that you are ready to let them back
in. It won't be easy, but it will be worth it.

Prayer

Dear God, I don't know how old some of
these secrets are and I don't know if I am
ready to talk and confess them to anyone.
Nonetheless, I know I can trust You, and I
recognize that this is a necessary step in my
healing journey. When the time is right, I
know You will give me the courage to con-
fide in someone who is trustworthy. Prepare

me and prepare that person. God, I know You are The Healer. You are merciful and forgiving. So today I trust You with the deepest things in my heart...

Homework

1. Think of a few people who love God and love you. Write them down in a list form. From there, circle the ones you trust most. Take the circled names and pray about who God is leading you to talk to. If you couldn't think of anyone right now, spend the rest of this week praying specifically about this. Pay close attention to the people you encounter at church, with your family, even at work. God always puts someone in our path to be a blessing.

People Who Love God and Me:

_____

_____

_____

_____

_____

_____

_____

Day 15
I Will Show You the Way

Psalm 32:8

8 I will instruct you and teach you in the way you should go; I will guide you with My eye.

It can definitely be terrifying to feel like you have lost control of your life. You may feel lost right now as you carry a luggage of worry on your back, but please know, God can take that burden from you if you'll surrender it. We have to look at this "losing control" thing as a good starting point. It is the first step in trusting God. We already know what happens when we try to take control of our own life without God. We fall hard. So, if we surrender and let God take control, we rest while having assurance that He will lead us in the way we should go. How do we do this? How do we let God take control? It is your decision today.

Every day you wake up, you have the choice to stress over how you're going to do things, or you can let go and let Him lead. He says He will teach us. Why would He need to teach us? It is obviously because we don't know the way. Why would He need to guide us? Because we are prone to getting lost.

Every day that you wake up, use this scripture in prayer. This scripture is God's promise talking to you. As a child of God, you can remind God of His promises. Not that He forgets, moreover, when we remind Him, we are actually reminding ourselves. Repeat His promises back to Him. Ask Him to instruct you and teach you in the way you should go.

The scripture says He will guide you with His eye. I used to wonder why it mentions God's eye. I came to realize that God sees everything and everyone. Not only that, but He sees the future. Who better to trust than the One True God who already knows your tomorrow, who already sees your future? He is the light, He is life, and He knows the way because He is the way.

Prayer

Dear God, Thank You for bringing me this far. Thank you for Your faithfulness. I admit, I do not know the way, therefore, I come before You, needing Your direction in my life. Your word says that You will show me the way. God, I want to be led in Your ways. I need Your guidance just like Your word says. Father, I know You are faithful to Your promises. Today, guide me, teach me, lead me. I surrender to You. I give you all my fears and insecurities. You know my hopes and dreams. I give those to You too. I surrender everything to You Lord. When I am tempted to stray, remind me that You are the Way, the Truth, and the Life. In the name of Jesus, I pray. Amen.

Questions for Reflection

1. Do you struggle with needing to feel in control most of the time?

2. What areas of your life are you having the most difficulty letting God lead?

Day 16
The Battlefield

Philippians 4:8

8 Finally, brethren, whatever things are true, whatever things are noble, whatever things are just, whatever things are pure, whatever things are lovely, whatever things are of good report, if there is any virtue and if there is anything praise-worthy--meditate on these things.

The mind is a major battlefield. It can dominate your emotions in a rollercoaster type of way, leaving you dizzy and out of control. Your mind can think of and create a complete conflict that does not exist in real life. Nonetheless, your emotions will react as if it did. Your mind can feed your fears, which in turn can control actions and further judgments. But who controls your mind? You do. You can allow it to run 100 miles an hour, or you can stop the thoughts before they gain control of you.

What are the thoughts that could be detrimental to you right now in the place where you find yourself? It could be thoughts of worthlessness, doubt, depression, thoughts of going back to something that hurt you, thoughts of hate, and the ones I despise most, the what-if thoughts. You cannot change the past, so why occupy your mind in the hamster wheel of what-ifs?

If your thoughts are causing you extra grief right now, why not take God's advice today? His word says to engage your thoughts in "whatever things are true, whatever things are noble, whatever things are just, whatever things are pure, whatever things are lovely..." This perfectly describes the Word of God.

You matter to God and He is taking care of you (Matthew 6:26-34). These are the things that you should meditate on and declare to the Lord in prayer. When we, as children of God, learn to redirect our thoughts to His Word, we take hold of the power He has given us, the power of a sound mind and self-control (2 Timothy 1:7).

Today, refocus your thoughts to mediate on His Word instead of the problems that you cannot fix. He will take care of the things that are out of your control.

Prayer

Dear God, I ask that You help me take control of my thoughts today. As I read Your Word, help me to store Your promises in my heart, that I may mediate on them when harmful thoughts want to settle in. I know I can trust You with my problems. I no longer want to worry about them. So, I give you control and ask that You would help me when I cannot help myself. Remind me of Your Word when I am weak and when negative thoughts want to control me. In the name of Jesus, I pray. Amen.

Questions for Reflection

1. Are there any "what-if's" that are taking up space in your thoughts today?

2. What scripture can you memorize to combat the negative thoughts that want to dwell in your mind?

Day 17
Wisdom to Live By

Proverbs 3:1-6

1 My son, do not forget my law, But let your heart keep my commands;
2 For length of days and long life And peace they will add to you.
3 Let not mercy and truth forsake you; Bind them around your neck, Write them on the tablet of your heart,
4 And so find favor and high esteem In the sight of God and man.
5. Trust in the LORD with all your heart, And lean not on your own understanding;
6. In all your ways acknowledge Him, And He shall direct your paths."

The Word of God is life to our mortal bodies. It is guidance to our wandering hearts. It is wisdom in our ignorance, and peace in our troubles. It is literally nutrition to our spiritual lives.

When I read these words in Proverbs, I see God's caring love for us. He wants peace for you and I. He desires long life for us. He even cares about His children finding favor in the eyes of man, which, let's be honest, is a huge convenience. He tells us how to achieve these important and beneficial things.

First of all, He reminds us not to forget His word, because in His word is where we find guidance and direction. It is so important that we keep it written in our hearts, literally memorizing simple but powerful key verses. Just by learning His Word and keeping His commandments, He promises us "length of days" and "peace." Who does not want a peaceful long life? The best part is, when God speaks about a long life, He is referring to eternal life. Sure, we might get a long life here on earth, but what really matters to Him, is our soul. To have eternal life with Jesus in His kingdom, that's the real prize.

The scriptures also speak about not forsaking mercy and truth. This is so important because we are the first to need God's mercy. Now that we have received it, we must also give it. God's order is for our own good. To do unto others as we want done unto us, benefits us. If we follow these words of wisdom we will find favor in the eyes of God and people. How beautiful that, not only does God care about our eternal lives, but He also wants us to have favorable lives here on earth.

We must not forget also to trust Him with all of our heart, bypassing our own understanding and wisdom. It's His guidance and wisdom that we must ask for and desire. When we do this, we can trust that He will direct our path.

Prayer

Dear God, Give me a love for Your Word. I want to live by it and meditate on it daily. Reveal Your Word to me and let it be my daily nutrition. Thank you caring and showing me the secret to a favorable and blessed life. I will carry truth and mercy within me everywhere I go. You loved me first and extended mercy to me, when I did not deserve it. Now, I will do the same unto others. Guide me and direct my steps. In the name of Jesus, I pray. Amen.

Questions for Reflection

1. Out of all the promises stated in the passages above, which one stands out the most to you?

2. Do you notice that before each promise there is an instruction? How practical or difficult is each instruction to you?

Day 18
The Value of a Friend

Ecclesiastes 4:9-12

9 Two are better than one, Because they have a good reward for their labor.
10 For if they fall, one will lift up his companion. But woe to him who is alone when he falls, For he has no one to help him up.
11 Again, if two lie down together, they will keep warm; But how can one be warm alone?
12 Though one may be overpowered by another, two can withstand him. And a threefold cord is not quickly broken.

I had not realized how many people I had pushed away during the time that I had been trapped in a destructive relationship, until it was all over. Starting with my parents and siblings, I began to see how I had been surrounded by people who loved me, yet I had been so consumed in an unwholesome relationship, investing all of my energy and time in trying to make it work, that I had left nothing for other people in my life.

I had some mending to do. It wasn't on purpose or with the intention of hurting anyone, it had just happened. Nonetheless, I understood that I had hurt people, while I myself was also hurting.

In some cases, I know it's different. A significant other can demand all of their partner's attention and time, and use abuse in order to forcefully isolate them from all family and friends. The person in this case has no fault, nonetheless reaps the same consequences of feeling isolated after the breakup. There is a reason the Word says, "Two are better than one." He knows we will have our weak moments. He knows we will need encouragement. There will be vulnerable moments where we will need friends to keep us accountable and focused on what matters, preventing us from slipping back into old tendencies.

He made us to dwell within relationships. That does not mean only romantic relationships. Do not neglect the people who surround you, who are waiting to care for and love you. If you have your parents, cultivate that relationship. It will serve you richly. If you have siblings, reach out to them. And don't make the mistake of overlooking the more mature in age. It could be that sweet elderly woman at your church, or your widowed neighbor, or even your grandmother. You may come to find a treasure of wisdom within them. Cherished friends come in all ages and from all different backgrounds.

Keep in mind, it is wise to take precautions and make sure you are investing in a relationship with someone who loves God and has a personal relationship with Him. Also, because of the vulnerability that comes after a breakup, seek trustworthy individuals who are of the same gender as you. That is not to say that you can't have friends who are non-Christian and of the opposite sex.

However, if you are seeking advice, encouragement, prayer, wisdom, and mentorship, it is best to find a strong, spiritual leader of your gender, who can be of spiritual edification.

Prayer

Dear God, Thank You for the people You have put in my life. At times I may not have appreciated them or taken them into account, but today I ask that You would help me rebuild relationships with my family and friends. I feel distant from many people, but I know You can change that. Put the right spiritual leaders in my path. Keep me safe from vulnerable situations that could lead me astray. I trust You Lord. In the name of Jesus, I pray. Amen

Questions for Reflection

1. Can you think of some important relationships that need mending and reconnection?

2. What are some steps you can take to get closer to the ones you have been far from?

Day 19
Declaring God's Truths

Isaiah 64:8

8 But now, O LORD, You are our Father; We are the clay, and You our potter; And all we are the work of Your hand.

Words do hurt. I remember the feeling of insults piercing my heart like steel cut arrows. I wasn't good enough, pretty enough, or smart enough for this man I thought loved me. After everything was said and done, I was left with an altered perception of myself. I could not hold eye contact with people. I could not accept a compliment. I saw myself as worthless. I felt disgusted being in my own body. It was shame, guilt, anger, and so many other emotions that hindered me from loving myself, and from seeing myself as the work of God's hand.

Perhaps you too find yourself feeling that way. Whether it was hurtful words that were thrown at you, or actions that made you feel this way, you need healing. You have to believe that God's Word is true. His Word says that you are the work of His hand. In other words, you are a work of art. And if

God is the One creating this art, no doubt it is extraordinary. He is molding you like clay, into who you need to be. The process is not always easy, but as long as you are in His hands, you can trust that you are safe. Not only that, but you are valuable. Sure, we all have flaws, we aren't perfect, but begin to accept yourself as God's precious work.

Reject the thoughts of pain and lies that come to tell you otherwise. Literally say it out loud. "I don't accept (lie). I am a beloved child of God." Hearing your own voice declare God's truths can help you begin to really believe it. The Bible confirms that our words are powerful. Use the power of God's Word to edify your life. Remember, you are the marvelous work of The Potter, our heavenly and perfect Father.

Prayer

Dear God, I believe Your Word is true. I know it will restore my life if I believe it. Today I decide to take Your Word as the absolute truth for my life. In the past I have allowed myself to believe lies about who I was and what I was worth. Now I know that I am valuable because You say I am. I am the work of Your hands, loved and carefully crafted. I trust that You are molding me into a complete masterpiece. I will trust the process and trust Your Word. Help me to always choose truth over lies. In the name of Jesus, I pray. Amen.

Questions for Reflection

1. Which lies have been the hardest for you to reject from your life?

2. Have you considered before the power of your words, and how will you begin to use that power for your personal healing?

Day 20
The Beauty of Clay

Philippians 3:13-14

*13 Brethren, I do not count myself to have appre-
hended; but one thing I do, forgetting those things
which are behind and reaching forward to those
things which are ahead,*
*14 I press toward the goal for the prize of the up-
ward call of God in Christ Jesus.*

Have you ever heard the expression "damaged
goods," referring to a person? Basically meaning,
someone who has become inferior, broken, dull, or
inadequate because of the things that have happened to them, or the things that they have done.
If someone in the Bible could have been given this
title by the Devil himself, it would have probably
been Rahab.

She was a harlot, in other terms, she was a pros-
titute. She was living in Jericho at the time when
God had commanded Joshua to destroy that city
along with all of its inhabitants. Because Rahab hid
two of Joshua's spies and saved their life, Joshua
had mercy on her and spared her life. In reality, if
we look at the big picture, it was God who was using

Joshua to save her. It wasn't only because she hid the spies. She also recognized God as the true God, and had enough courage to ask to be saved along with her family. Her past did not matter at that point. Her acknowledgment of God and her faith allowed God to change her situation, saving her and her family.

She was never the same after that and her identity changed. She became part of the God's people, playing a very important role in history. From her descendants came King David, and eventually The Son of God in the flesh, Jesus Christ.

Like Rahab, it's time to leave your past behind and strive for God's plans and ways. The identity that the world gave you is nullified by the new identity you have in Christ. He makes all things new. It's time to forget those things which are behind and reach forward to those things which are ahead. Don't look back. He has better things in store for you.

Prayer

Dear God, I want to leave so many things behind. Hurt, shame, regrets. Help me to move on from these things. I know You have great things in store for me. I trust You with my story. I am not damaged goods, I am a child of God, loved and bought with the precious blood of Jesus. Let me not forget these truths when the enemy wants to bring me down. I want to move forward and stop dwelling on the past. Help me in my weak moments.   In the name of Jesus, I pray. Amen.

Questions for Reflection

1. Before you surrendered to God where did your identity come from?

2. What are some ways you can keep yourself focused on your goals, rather than the mistakes and failures of the past?

Day 21
Forgiveness

Matthew 6:14-15

*14 "For if you forgive men their trespasses, your
heavenly Father will also forgive you.
15 But if you do not forgive men their trespasses,
neither will your Father forgive your trespasses.*

It has taken us 21 days to get to this topic. We have
already discussed accepting God's forgiveness for
ourselves. Today, however, it's about rendering
the forgiveness we have received to someone else,
someone who does not deserve it.

You see, none of us deserved God's forgiveness.
We have all sinned countless times, in so many different ways. There was no possible way to earn
God's forgiveness. Yet in His infinite mercy, He offered us the incomparable gift of forgiveness and
salvation. If you really take the time to think about
this, it is something too great to wrap your mind
around. But God did not leave us without responsibility.

Jesus states in the New Testament that the greatest two commandments are to love God and love
each other (Mat 22:37-39). We love Him because

He first loved us (1 John 4:19), and now we forgive because He first forgave us. Jesus clearly teaches about the importance of forgiveness. He unapologetically stated that forgiving others is necessary in order for God to forgive us. That might not be everyone's favorite verse in the Bible.

Why is the standard so high? Because the price was so high. If Jesus paid the highest possible price to be able to offer us complete forgiveness, who are we not to forgive another human being, who like us, is faulty and prone to make mistakes?

You may have many reasons why a certain person, or more than one, does not deserve an ounce of forgiveness. But in God's eyes, it's not an excuse. I believe forgiving someone is first beneficial for you, before it ever affects them.

When you forgive, you let go of that person as your controller. That person no longer has the power to control your emotions towards them, to dictate your actions, to consume your thoughts. When you forgive, you free yourself from holding on to burdens that you should not carry.

When you make the choice to forgive, the other person may not even be aware. They may or may not even care. Maybe they haven't even asked for forgiveness. The act of forgiving them may actually never affect them personally, but it will always affect you.

In obedience we forgive, and as a result, we reap the reward. Forgiveness and freedom!

Prayer

Dear God, Thank You for Your gift of forgiveness. I understand I didn't deserve it, yet in Your mercy You sent Your Son Jesus to die on the cross to save me. Now, I understand I also need to be forgiving because Your Word commands it. I ask that You would help me to forgive this person. I want to obey Your Word and that means I must forgive and let go of any grudges. Today I choose to forgive _____. I let go of any resentment. It's not mine to hold onto. I let go of revengeful or negative thoughts towards this person. Although they have hurt me, they are still Your creation and You love them. I ask that You would bless them, save them, direct their path. Help me to forgive each day that I wake up. Help me to pray for them when I feel like speaking against them. I no longer want to carry the burden of unforgiveness. You have made me free and I will walk in Your freedom. In the name of Jesus. Amen.

Questions for Reflection

1. Are there any individuals in your life whom you are still withholding forgiveness from?

2. Search your heart and ask yourself, what are the reasons you are having a hard time forgiving?

Day 22
Death and Life

Proverbs 18:21

*21 Death and life are in the power of the tongue,
And those who love it will eat its fruit.*

Our words have so much more power than what we give them credit for. Sometimes we think that spoken words simply vanish into thin air once they have been uttered. The truth is, spoken words are much more than just sounds. The Bible gives great importance to our words. Here are just a few examples.

> *Matthew 12:36 says, "But I say to you that for every idle word men may speak, they will give account of it in the day of judgment. For by your words you will be justified, and by your words you will be condemned."*

> *Proverbs 15:4 says, "A wholesome tongue is a tree of life, but perverseness in it breaks the spirit."*

We have the power to build up our own lives by speaking life, by declaring blessings, and by rebuking negative words spoken against us.

Sometimes you have to lead with your words before your even believe it in your heart. We know that the heart can be unstable, so you must not depend on what you feel.

Lead with the power from the Word of God. Look in the mirror and tell yourself that God has made you more than a conqueror through Jesus Christ (Rom 8:37). On those painful days when you feel weak, unable to see past the fear and insecurity, remind yourself audibly that God's strength is made perfect in your weakness (2 Cor 12:9). When shame wants to creep in again and make itself at home, declare that He has cast your sins into the depths of the ocean and will not remember than anymore (Micah 7:19). When the world tries to tell you of all the reasons why you can't, remember that Jesus already overcame the world (John 16:33). So, whose word will you accept?

His word has power, if we believe it. The words that come out of our mouth have authority. They can build us up or tear us down. Be wise with the words you choose. Don't put yourself down, even in small ways. If you make a mistake, don't call yourself dumb. If you did not get a certain job, don't say "I'll never get a good job." If you feel like the healing journey is dragging, don't say, "I'll never get over my ex."

Use your words to declare strength, to declare life. God gave us His word which is full of abundant life. Declare His truths, instead of the Devil's lies.

You are healing.

You are moving forward.

You are succeeding.

God is fulfilling His purposes in your life. Believe it!

Prayer

Dear God, Your Word is life. You have given me a voice to declare Your Word and use it for strength. Forgive me if I have used my words carelessly. I no longer want to speak idle words. I want to use my voice to declare Your promises over my life. I can overcome and be victorious because of Jesus who already overcame the world. You are my protection. I am safe in You. You are making me whole. Thank You for Your mercy. Your love is everlasting. Remind me of Your promises when I am weak. In the name of Jesus, I pray. Amen.

Homework

1. Write down a list of Gods biblical promises for your life. Every morning as you wake up and have your prayer time with God, incorporate reading these scriptures and saying these declarations aloud. The more you say it and memorize it, the easier it is to believe. And when we believe, it's an open invitation for God to work in our lives and bless us.

2. Read James 1:6-7. What does the Word say about unbelief and how it affects our prayers?

Day 23
Chosen

1 Corinthians 1:27

27 But God has chosen the foolish things of the world to put to shame the wise, and God has chosen the weak things of the world to put to shame the things which are mighty;

I felt like the weakest of them all, and afraid like I had no idea I could fear. I felt inadequate and unprepared to be a mother, a single mother. But after many tears and battles within myself and with God, I opened my heart to the courage He had been offering me all along. I chose life, and in my weakness, He showed me His strength. He brought me through impossible circumstances. He made a way through the darkest of tunnels, and He comforted me when I felt too broken to go on.

Have you ever felt weak, vulnerable, like everyone around you has the gift of confidence and courage except for you? God understands. In reality, that's a great place to start. When we recognize our weaknesses and limitations, we can understand why we would need to depend on something greater than our own strength. God does not need us, yet He chose us. We are His vessels, made to reflect His love, and live for Him. For God, no resume is needed, nor a background check, because Lord knows we could never be good enough. He chooses us simply because He loves us.

Now it's up to you to accept His calling in your life. Yes, you may feel weak, but God can take it from there. As the scripture says, God has chosen the weak things of this world to put to shame the things which are mighty (1 Corinthians 1:27).

As long as you have a willing heart, you don't have to worry about being good enough. He will delight in using your life for His glory.

Prayer

Dear God, Thank You for accepting me as I am. You are aware of my weaknesses and shortcomings, yet You still love me and have a purpose for my life. I surrender all of my fears and doubts to You. Use me for Your glory. Let my story be evidence of Your mercy and love. I no longer want to define myself by my abilities, of what I can and cannot do. I want to see myself as You see me. In the name of Jesus, I pray. Amen

Questions for Reflection

1. What are some of the weaknesses in your life that you feel may be preventing you from growing spiritually?

2. What are some of the strengths that you desire to have?

Day 24
No Turning Back

Galatians 5:1

1 Stand fast therefore in the liberty by which Christ has made us free, and do not be entangled again with a yoke of bondage.

The Lord has done a great work in your life. He has freed you from guilt and shame, forgiven you for all of your sins, and adopted you into His family. Yet, no doubt there are days when we will feel the weight of our past again? I speak for myself because I have had plenty these moments.

We live in a world that is still governed by darkness. To a certain extent, the world is the Devil's territory (John 14:30). Knowing this, we must understand that we are not completely exempt from Satan's attacks. The Bible reveals that he is the accuser (Rev 12:10). He would love to see you trapped again, bound in chains, living in the past. He wants to keep you dwelling on the memories, wasting your time and energy on the what-ifs.

If the Lord is freeing you from a toxic relationship, from guilt, from low self-esteem, from sexual immorality, and other things, do not give room for the Devil's accusations or schemes to take you back into that life. Recognize these attacks are from the enemy and remember what Jesus has done for you. He has given you liberty. Grasp the beauty of this freedom and stand in it. In the hard times, declare it, claim it. Don't let your mind occupy itself in the accusations, in the regrets, or even in missing the days of bondage.

More than likely you will have soul-ties to the person you are trying to heal from, especially if there was sexual intimacy in the relationship. It is normal to experience withdrawal pains when you are letting go. Nonetheless, it does not have to keep you in bondage. The Lord is healing you, so be careful not to take steps backwards, giving too much thought to the past relationship. It is time to live in the freedom that God has given you.

Prayer

Dear God, You have given me freedom. I no longer want to feel the weight of guilt from my past. I don't want to give ear to the voice of the accuser. You are my Helper and Deliverer. I will put my trust in You. Break the soul-ties that have been formed with the wrong people. My heart does not belong to them. It belongs to You. Break negative attachments that I have formed. Guard my heart and mind in Christ Jesus. Let Your peace flow in my life. In the name of Jesus, I pray. Amen

Questions for Reflection

1. Do you struggle with entertaining thoughts of your past relationship?

2. How does dwelling on these thoughts affect the way you are healing?

3. Are you willing to take these thoughts captive by submitting them to God as soon as they enter your mind?

Day 25
Blessings from Pain

Genesis 50:20

20 But as for you, you meant evil against me; but God meant it for good, in order to bring it about as it is this day, to save many people alive.

The truth is, we can all point at someone in our life who has caused us pain, intentionally or not. This scripture is found within the pages of the story of Joseph, a boy who was sold into slavery by his own brothers who hated him. Talk about evil. His early life was full of suffering, from being sold into human trafficking, to having false accusations of attempted rape charged against him. He knew what it felt like to have evil plotted against him.

Through all this, however, Joseph allowed God to work in his life, and eventually he saw God's plan unravel. The time came when he had the ultimate chance to take revenge against his brothers because of the position of power he had been given. He instead took that opportunity to show mercy and forgiveness, astoundingly declaring, "You meant evil against me; but God meant it for good." I believe

85

we can look back on our lives and see how God has brought beauty from the pain we have faced.

In my personal life, I have seen the best gifts come out of the darkest season in my life. After leaving the toxic relationship I had been in for 4 years, I was left to pick up the pieces of my life, alone, too ashamed to ask anyone for help. Soon after the breakup, I found out I was pregnant. At the time, it seemed like the worst situation I could have possibly been in.

Now, I realize that the child God gifted me during that time was the most beautiful and timely gift I could have ever received. I see that the hurt and heartache that I went through, actually led me to the most beautiful place in my life. It brought me to my knees and led me to Jesus. I have grown so much spiritually and learned true dependence on God. What the Devil meant for evil against me, God turned it into something amazing. But I had to choose to let God mold me. I knew it was easier to slip back into old habits, and let shame keep me from God and His plans. Because of this I determined myself to cling to God. I am forever grateful for the process that led me to where I am today.

Surely, you can identify many things that the Devil meant for the destruction of your life. But know that those same things that were meant to break you, God can turn them into blessings and make you stronger in the process. I pray that you would allow Him to continue turning your pain into beauty.

Prayer

Dear God, Thank You for bringing healing into my life. I know there were many hurts in my heart caused by people that I loved. I forgive them. Now I just ask that You continue to help me heal. Help me forgive them when I want to hold resentment against them. Allow me to give mercy instead of seeking revenge. Turn my pain into joy. In the name of Jesus, I pray. Amen.

Questions for Reflection

1. Looking at Joseph's life in the scriptures, how do you feel you would have reacted if you were in his place and you had the chance to either forgive or take revenge?

2. Are you beginning to see small ways in which God is bringing the good out of the painful things you've been through? If you can't identify those things just yet, be patient and ask Him to allow you to see a small part of what He is doing behind the scenes.

Day 26
Greater Things
Are Yet to Come

Haggai 2:9

9 The glory of this latter temple shall be greater than the former,' says the LORD of hosts. 'And in this place I will give peace,' says the LORD of hosts."

I remember feeling like it was the end. Surely, I had no good future to look forward to. I was pregnant and alone, all while in the middle of trying to get a degree. I was living a double life that was about to be exposed by my growing baby-bump. I thought I had reached God's max point of forgiveness, not to mention, my parents', as well.

When the truth finally came out, I was broken for my sin and the pain I had caused so many people as a result of my choices. Even after I was offered forgiveness and love by my parents and church family, I continued believing that God's calling for my life had been nullified. I was so humbled to just receive forgiveness, that I did not expect to ever be used by God again. But through my healing journey, God put wonderful people in my life who spoke truth to me, who held me accountable, who did not let me stay down. And one day, as I was seeking the Lord in prayer, I opened my Bible and began to read the book of Haggai. Then this scripture boldly stood out to me, and I understood.

A set-back, a bump in the road, a detour, is not the end of God's plan for your life. It's an opportunity for growth and for God's glory to be shown. The process is difficult, but the end result is beautiful. You will have hard times, commit mistakes, and feel pain, but God will fulfill His promises in you. Nothing you have been through will be in vain.

We can learn and grow from each hardship that we have endured. And we can let the Lord restore our temple to a greater formation than it was before.

Prayer

Dear God, I trust that You are restoring me and making me stronger than I was before. I believe the experiences You have allowed me to go through, will serve greater purposes. I am learning to trust You, depend on You, and so much more. You will not leave me unfinished. Instead, I know the latter temple will be greater than the former. I am open to Your will. Lead me today. In the name of Jesus, I pray. Amen.

Questions for Reflection

1. Have you felt like you've come to the end of a dream, a calling, a talent?

2. What are some steps you can take to reinvest yourself in your God-given dreams and goals?

3. Are you expecting God to restore you to an even better temple than you were before, or are you limiting God with doubts and low expectations?

Day 27
Write the Vision

Habakkuk 2:2-3

2 Then the LORD answered me and said: "Write the vision And make it plain on tablets, That he may run who reads it.
3 For the vision is yet for an appointed time; But at the end it will speak, and it will not lie. Though it tarries, wait for it; Because it will surely come, It will not tarry.

Before you get into your car to drive, you have to know where you are headed. Before you purchase a plane ticket, you have to know your destination. It is the same in life. You must have your eyes set in a specific direction before making decisions and choosing paths.

The Lord gives us the tools we need to succeed, to heal, to grow, but we must know what we are aiming for. In Proverbs 4:26 it says to "ponder the path of your feet and let all your ways be established." Our first clearly defined goal must be to walk in the Lords ways, following His commandments. We cannot have success if we are not in His will. We must also have day to day practical goals.

Things like decluttering our mind and physical space. Going to sleep early. Taking walks. Tackling tasks one at a time.

For me it was small things at first like ridding my surroundings of junk, emotionally and physically. I cleaned out old memories, I threw away sentimental cards and items that I had held onto for years. It was time to move on. Then my next goal was to go back to school and get my degree. I prayed about it, set goals, and God opened doors. I was able to accomplish that and so much more once I applied God's wisdom to my everyday life.

Whatever it is that you wish to accomplish, put it before the Lord in prayer, then take action to get there.

Write out a plan. Don't worry about time, it will pass anyway. Start today by writing down your goals, not vaguely but detailed. God has given us all different talents and abilities. But we can't accomplish much by just wishing and putting it off another day. I love the wisdom in this scripture. If we write down our goals, they become an inspiration to run with. And when the motivation wears off, your words on paper will not change. They will remind you of where you were headed in the first place. When you write down your vision for that year or even that month, keep it within reading distance, up on your wall, on your bathroom mirror, or someplace where you know you will encounter it daily. You will be amazed at the results once you start putting God's Word into practice. Pray that God will open the right doors and give you peace about the goals you are setting.

Prayer

Dear God, I have these goals and dreams that I have put off way too long. I know the talents and abilities You have given me are for a purpose. I pray that You would guide the decisions I will make in the days and months to come. I put my plans in Your hands. These are my plans... Open the right doors for me and close the doors that are not for me. I will write the vision and make it plain on paper. Help me find a starting point. In the name of Jesus, I pray. Amen.

Questions for Reflection

1. Are there any goals that you've set for yourself multiple times but have not yet achieved?

2. Have you ever written them down? How about writing them now?

3. Do you have a plan on how you're going to reach those goals? Start today.

Day 28
True Beauty

Proverbs 31:30

30 Charm is deceitful and beauty is passing, But a woman who fears the LORD, she shall be praised.

As women, we have the temptation to focus a little too much on our outward appearance. This can be especially significant if we want to prove to someone that we are worth more than they treated us to be. I understand, I tried to compensate for all the times I was made to feel unworthy. At times, I put more importance on my outward appearance, while ignoring the bitterness growing within. I brought myself to believe that if I had looked better on the outside, then my ex-partner would have loved me and would have tried to make the relationship work.

It is an easy lie to believe and to act upon. But the truth is, a man who is not truly surrendered to the Lord, cannot truly love a woman the way Christ expects. Therefore, at any given time he can fall into unfaithfulness, become bored of a relationship, even abuse and hurt the woman he claims to love. None of that is your fault, and your beauty could not have stopped his actions.

At times our response is to be angry with ourselves for the way we look, and blame ourselves for the other person's actions. This response is damaging to us emotionally and mentally. We must see ourselves the way God sees us.

It is okay to try to be healthy and take care of our outward appearance, but everything should be done in moderation. Be careful to not have the wrong intentions. Don't invest your energy in trying to be beautiful in order to "show him what he lost." Instead use that energy to work on inner beauty. If you want to set goals for fitness and health, do it for yourself and for the temple of the Holy Spirit. Ask God to help you build your self-esteem and to give you godly confidence. Work on forgiveness and kindness. Outward beauty will waste away with the years, but a woman with a God-fearing heart will still radiate beauty.

Prayer

Dear God, Make me beautiful. Take away any bitterness and unforgiveness that is staining my inner beauty. Help me build my confidence and self-esteem. I am loved by You. Help me believe this truth. I let go of the lies that say I am not good enough or pretty enough. I am enough for my Father in Heaven. Complete me and continue working me. Cleanse me of any inward blemishes. I want to be a woman who fears the

Lord, who follows His word, and radiates true beauty. In the name of Jesus, I pray. Amen.

Questions for Reflection

1. Do you at times put more effort into your outward beauty rather than your inward beauty?

2. Have your past experiences made it difficult for you to feel beautiful?

3. Are you blaming your outward flaws on any abuse you have received in the past?

Day 29
Learning to be Content

Hebrews 13:5

5 Let your conduct be without covetousness; be content with such things as you have. For He Himself has said, "I will never leave you nor forsake you."

As you continue through your journey, there will be times when you will encounter people who are where you wish to be. It may seem that you find yourself surrounded by people who are in great relationships, some anticipating marriage, others with your dream career, and then there are those who just seem happy and successful no matter where they are or what they are doing.

Do not let this be a cause for frustration or regret. Everyone is fighting their own battles and walking their own journey. No one has it all figured out. No one is living the perfect life. Instead of asking why and wishing things would have turned out differently in your life, embrace the changes, and look forward to the greater things God has in store for you.

Learning to be content has been one of the hardest struggles for me. When I take my eyes off God and begin to focus on what I wish I had, or how I could have done things differently, I find myself in an unproductive pity party. As children of God, we have access to the most priceless gifts. Sure, material things are good, but nothing material can compare to the peace of God. His new mercy every morning and the assurance that He is with us, is more valuable than any earthly luxury. These are the things that matter.

God knows what we need. He wants us to trust Him to provide the material things as well. But while you wait for whatever it is you are praying for, learn to be content in the place where He has you.

Every season of life has a purpose given by God. He has already written your story in His book. Trust His plan, and you will see a beautiful story begin to unravel.

Prayer

Dear God, I ask for your help today. I want to feel content, because there are so many things I wish I could change. The past is gone, now I am here, and I need You. I don't want to wallow in regret and feel jealous of others. I don't want to put my eyes on other people. I want to keep my eyes on You. You have written my story and I know I should trust You. Help me to embrace this season in my life and live it to the fullest in You Lord. When I start to sink in hopelessness, pick me up again. Remind me that You are with me. You will never leave me nor forsake me. Thank you, God. In the name of Jesus, I pray. Amen.

Questions for Reflection

1. In what area of your life has it been the hardest to find contentment?

2. Do you find that you often compare yourself to others and wish you had what they have?

Day 30
Trusting His Ways

Isaiah 55:8-9

8 "For My thoughts are not your thoughts, Nor are your ways My ways," says the LORD.
9 "For as the heavens are higher than the earth, So are My ways higher than your ways, And My thoughts than your thoughts.

It may seem frightening to trust God when you feel He is asking you to let go of certain things. It might be plans, ideas, even people, that you have held on to for a long time, that you are now being asked to surrender.

When you initially "let go," it may feel like you are grieving a loss, because in a way it is like a death. It is the death of a dream to be happy with that particular person. The death of your plans to be this or have that by a certain age. The death of your will and your ways.

I wanted to be married by age 25. I always said it and I had marked it in my calendar years before. When I was 24, I was a new mom trying to cope with single parenting a toddler, going back to school, and trying to keep somewhat of a social life to avoid isolation and falling into depression. There was no boyfriend in the scene, not even the prospects of one.

Realistically, I knew I could not be married by 25. I literally had to grieve the loss of that expectation. It was painful, not really because of the timeline I had, but more because I did not know if it would ever happen. I did not know if it was in God's plans for me. I had to let it go, trusting that God had my life in His hands and that His ways were higher than mine.

It may be a difficult process to begin. Nevertheless, I encourage you today to begin trusting God with that which you are still reserving from Him. You can trust that He has better things in store. I know you may feel hesitant and even protective of your own ways, your own ideas and plans, but today God is reminding you, "So are my ways higher than yours, and my thoughts than your thoughts." One day you will be able to look back and realize that it was all more than worth it.

Prayer

Dear God, You know the things that I have held back from You. It's frightening to let them go because I don't know the future. I know that Your ways are higher than mine, but You understand that it is painful to let go of certain things. Please comfort me through this process. You are my comforter. Break down the walls I have built. You can have everything. I no longer want to give myself partially to You. You can have all of me. In the name of Jesus, I pray. Amen.

Questions for Reflection

1. Are there certain things or people that God is asking you to surrender to Him?

2. How does it feel to give something over to God without really knowing what will happen?

3. Do you trust that God has higher ways and thoughts for your life than you have for your-self?

An Encouraging Word from the Author

Thank you, dear reader, for taking the time to read these special thoughts from my heart. I pray that you continue to seek God and fall in love with His word every day. This is just the beginning of the work God will be doing in your life. Trust Him with the process. You will never regret it. My desire is that you find your value and identity in God, so that you will be brave enough to wait for what you deserve and walk away from detrimental relationships. Never forget that you are strong, you are valuable, and you are loved.

Vasti

ABOUT THE AUTHOR

Vasti Loredo is a devoted mother, a loving daughter, and a toxic relationship survivor. Her experience of acknowledging and escaping from a toxic relationship with her son gives her great insight into the plight of others.

Vasti is a certified Christian Life Coach and alumni of Master Life Coach Training Institute. She also works as a Registered Nurse. She is active in her church teaching youth groups and working with younger teenage girls. She loves participating in her worship team on Sundays either singing or playing her keyboard.

She is an author and speaker and lives in Midland, Texas with her son, Jonathan.

SUGGESTED RESOURCES

DeMoss, Nancy Leigh, *Choosing Forgiveness: Your Journey to Freedom*, Chicago, IL: Moody Publishers, 2008.

Gresh, Dannah, *And the Bride Wore White: Seven Secrets to Sexual Purity*, Chicago, IL: Moody Publishers, 2012.

OTHER RESOURCES BY VASTI LOREDO

Vasti is available to speak at women's groups, youth groups, and in Life Coach training sessions. She is fluent in both English and Spanish. She offers valuable insights and is available to speak on the following topics:
- Overcoming Toxic Relationships
- Purity
- Single Adulthood
- Single Motherhood
- Growing Your Relationship with God
- Discovering Your God Given SHAPE
- ... and more

How to Connect with Vasti

If you would like to schedule Vasti for your event or for Life Coaching you are invited to contact her at:

Email: lifecoachvasti@gmail.com

Or on Facebook

www.facebook.com/Life-Coaching-with-Vasti-107857431067944/

Or in her private Facebook group for those in toxic relationships: @To Be Complete

LEAVE A WELL

Someone said, "When you go through the valley, leave a well." In other words, when Christians go through difficult times and experience God's help and strength, we ought to leave a source of blessing for those travelers who will come behind us.

If this little devotional book has been a blessing to you, please consider taking a few moments to leave a "Review" at site where you purchased this book. Leaving a review of at least 25 words will help others find this book.

You can follow this link to leave a review for *To Be Complete* at Amazon.

FRANKLIN PUBLISHING

The goal of Franklin Publishing is to enable Pastors, Evangelists, Missionaries, and Christian leaders and presenters to become published authors. Becoming a published author expands your influence and builds your ministry. You can write the book or sermon series which God has laid on your heart. We can walk that road with you. Start by downloading our free writers publishing guide.

www.FranklinPublishing.org

Come and visit our Facebook page and be sure to like and follow us to keep up with writing tips and new developments.

www.facebook.com/FranklinPublishing

FRANKLIN
PUBLISHING

www.ingramcontent.com/pod-product-compliance
Lightning Source LLC
Chambersburg PA
CBHW052053270326
41931CB00012B/2741